Home-Front Passage

Home-Front Passage

A Southern Sojourn with Monologues

Donegan Smith

Academy Press
Hickory, North Carolina

Copyright © 2007 Donegan Smith
All rights reserved.

Published by Academy Press
2951 – 7th St. Dr. NE
Hickory, NC 28601

Except for brief excerpts in articles or critical reviews, no part of this book may be reproduced in any form by any means, electronic, mechanical, recorded, photocopy, or otherwise, without prior permission in writing from the copyright owner.

Cover design by Philip Blosser/Lulu.com

Printed in the United States of America
ISBN 978-0-6151-5716-0

PREFACE

    This is basically a true story and a rite of passage for a southern boy caught in the middle of his parents' strained and confusing marriage.

    The monologues give voice to the people and a particular stage-play nuance and vibe.

    A very special and heart-felt debt of thanks to Dr. Philip Blosser for his faith and belief in this work. My gratitude also to Ms. Beverly Hefner, who transcribed the manuscript into its present form, as well as to Ms. Elizabeth Flow for her contribution as copy editor.

Donegan Smith
July 7, 2007

HOME FRONT PASSAGE

It was Halloween morning and, in sharp lower back pain, I wondered about the ultimate trick or treat. The question is: do you remember your birth? People have clearly recalled dying and returning from "the other side," but what about *entering* this most perfect of worlds? I made a little entrance during the time President Roosevelt was trying to get us all to stop "matriculating in a school for the blind," as Tennessee Williams nailed it so perfectly in *The Glass Menagerie*.

The late thirties in rural, tobacco-farming, North Carolina was hard times for all who had gutted it out since 1933. It was a time to see the Light and enjoy some salvation. The rumblings in Europe meant nothing to my people. No one gave a plu-perfect damn about that paper-hanging, "Kem-Tone Klown" – Little Adolph. All of the hard-scrabble farmers just wanted to survive ... and keep faith with the land.

Well ... I did. I survived, and I swear I remember somewhere deep ... darkly deep, I remember coming into this world.

On a cold, April morning, in a tiny four-room house about thirty miles from Raleigh, my Mother got into trouble during her seventh month. Dad was shaking the windows snoring – afflicted with White Lightening. My Grandmother, whom I would later call "Two-Mamas," was there, and I wanted to see the Light. Only problem was – I was twisted and Momma was in a world of hurt. My Daddy was revived somehow and dispatched to get old Doc Young. Trouble was the good doctor had been my Daddy's drinking partner the night before. No matter ... Daddy would get them both straightened out and ready for duty. Even Mother admired his healing, soothing ways ... you see my Daddy had desperately wanted to be a doctor.

There we were – all of us frustrated and in panic because, you see, I was breech. Mother was not cooperating in my need to come into the world – backwards! Yeah.... I would hear the refrain all too often: "Yes, he was seven months and breech and he's been backwards ever since."

It was a good thing my Daddy read medical books for recreation because Doc Young, shaking hands and all, was losing Momma. Finally, he made some innovative move, at Daddy's urging, and plop! Backwards ... but out I came, all three and a half pounds of bloody mess. Two-Mamas screamed when Momma passed out from the severe bleeding and the doctor yelled: "Make haste, Freeman, make haste. We're losing this brave woman! Put the boy down, he's dead. He didn't make it through ... come on now, help with this bleeding!"

Daddy kissed my slippery head and then there was cold from the metal table. From the liquid, soothing warmth to piercing cold ... all in one instant!

Now ... we've all had anger ... maybe even choking anger, and my little belly was full of it – but no sound could give it voice. Finally, on his way to get boiled cloths from the wood stove, Daddy put his gentle fingers on my belly button, and I heaved up an angry burst of breath and Daddy yelled: "He's alive, by Christ, my boy's alive! Clear his passages, Doc – I'll mind my Mabel. Doc, do it now!"

Well, three and a half pounds isn't much to scream with, but I showed them that my lungs worked just fine. It was not enough, but my Daddy had a plan to save my pre-mature ass. He got a cigar box, lined it with cotton, told Two-Mamas to smear lard all over me, then he lit the stove, propped the oven door open with a stick and there I was – safely incubating into this world and everybody praying I would still be breathing later on, after the long ride to the nearest hospital.

We both made it! But I swear problems started between me and Momma from the git-go. Ever wonder at what exact messy moment all the problems within a family get started? Momma thought that I almost killed her and, you're damned right, I – Donald Max – felt lost and angry, having been thrown away "dead" and cold ... and nothing.

We also made it out of the grayness of the thirties and into the light of the forties. England was "on her knees," to hear my great Uncle Kirky tell it. He was some kind of World War I hero, and even as 'wee' as I was – he let me hold his Army pistol and play "swordfight" with his old bayonet. Uncle Kirky smoked Camels and coughed like hellfire itself, and I never knew what they all whispered about when something called Mustard Gas was mentioned. One day, through perfect smoke rings, Uncle Kirky said:

UNCLE KIRKY

Now that we've come through to 1940, we can't make the mistake of messin' with Germany again. Plague take 'em! Let England get brains for once – sorriest, silliest ... and strangest damned mess of people I've ever seen. Any man that will put down his confounded tea cup in muddy, cesspool of a trench, blow his tinny, little whistle, and send over half of his men to instant death – charging with only a swagger stick in his hand – deserves to fight *on his own*. Now, believe it, they'd come back to the trench headquarters, with thousands of men's blood on their hands ... and, I swear, I heard this one prissy Brit say: "Say, old boy, you Yank there, do you have any sugar and milk about? Tea is so uncivilized without proper sugar and milk, you know." Well ... I opened his head up with a can of milk and never looked a man's son of 'em in the eye again. No ... not now son, no more. It's your bedtime. You've got to help us in the fields tomorrow ... bring us that clear, well water when we're parched. Good night, Little Donny Max, sleep tight ... and have peaceful dreams, ol' son.

I was safe and secure and worried over at Two-Mamas and Papa's farm ... my Mother's home. I wondered if I'd ever be "special" ... special enough to be a soldier and kill Germans and laugh at the English? Just before sleep, I overheard some loud talk about "holding our own, keep our own safe and not messin' with the Japs unless they, by God, invade us and storm the beach at Kitty Hawk!" I then dreamed of low-flying fighter planes and huge ships bobbing and weaving through blue, blue waters and fiery-red suns all over the sky ... and I was safe and the only grandchild ... and I wondered about my Daddy ... we were going into 1941 and where was my Daddy?

He was working somewhere, wiring houses. I knew he was a crack electrician and had passed the licensing board at seventeen, having quit school in the eighth grade. Someday my Daddy might show me how he was the fastest telephone pole climber in all of Harnett County, North Carolina:

DADDY

Now, Son, don't ever fail to have respect for electricity. It's a joy to have and a comfort, but she's also a mean, wild lady with a wicked bite ... so you respect the bitch. I don't know, Son, they just do ... hurricanes and such get names after women too. Lightening is so purdy up in the sky, but you better respect the power. Well ... now most natural disasters are named after women and, believe me, you'll understand someday. Hell, the next bad storm off Roanoke Island could be called "Mabel" after your Momma in yonder. Never mind now ... you'll find a way to understand someday. Here's a nickel – go get you a Baby Ruth.

That made me go crazy inside because no one would ever tell me things or explain what was really going on. I remember telling our old, yeller dog, Trixie, that I guess this skinny, sickly, three-and-a-half-pounder with lard on his ass would always have to learn about life and people very slowly ... and always the hard way.

One thing I did sense early on was that my Momma and Daddy couldn't live with each other or stay apart either. Anybody else ever been caught in the middle of that little "tap dance"? Daddy loved to stay away and work so he could drink and laugh and tell stories in bars and Momma loved being at her home place where everyone agreed that Daddy was her "big mistake" and "Christian cross to bear" and that his drinking was a sure road to hell and would shame all in the Baptist clans of our very "dry" Harnett County.

So ... there was this angry pull in me. I loved my Daddy and wanted him with me and to show me how to do things with my hands. But you also have to please the ones you're with – so I would sit beautifully behaved in church because I was my mother's "miracle from God" and I would be her good boy simply because I was alive ... can we have an "Amen"?

Daddy came home sick with flu and whiskey, I reckon, and it was so exciting to hear the men talk about some mysterious "rumors of war". England simply could not hold out according to Daddy and we just had to get into it. He wanted to be a soldier or sailor so bad. Being a good electrician and having a family was never even close to being enough for him. I wondered if it was ever enough for any man.

Daddy got better, and I noticed that he and Momma did go into their bedroom together at night. I shared a bedroom too—right off the kitchen. It had a feather bed, an old dresser, a Slop Jar (there was no indoor plumbing) and mainly it had Billy Ray. He was my uncle but only six years older than me and I never could get that straight in my head. Now, in Billy Ray's head, he had some bad electrical currents. Daddy loved him a lot but did tell me that Billy had some "shorted circuits" ... you see my roommate and playmate was brain damaged:

BILLY RAY

Dunnud, you are, ain't you? Huddee! I know you're one, Dunnud, you'd be one of dem ... aggerbaitin ones that would ride on any uggy blame tractor if you could. Mules is the onliest way to work so you hush you mawf. You better' nebber climb on one of dem machines 'round me 'cause I'll wear you slam out with a corn stalk and tell my Daddy you're one of 'dem! You'd be worse than Uncle Kirky's crazy boy, David K. You're little and puny and your Momma, Sister Mabel, dresses you purdy on Sunday for church ... and I ain't nebber going' in there. I'll always be sittin' in the car and then git "Black" chockee ice cream and you git sissy "niller-white", and then I git to ride home on the runnin' board and you have to stay purdy for Mabel, so there. I ... I wonder if I could ... I want a big, bell-bustin' Pepsi with peanuts floating in it ... I'm sick of putting all of that sugar in my ice tea ... I want some ... I wonder if'n I still have my birfday money hid in the corn crib? I'll see now, and you better nebber, ebber be a slab-sided lazy bone 'round me 'cause ... well there, I done tolt you!

And so went my days on the farm with Billy Ray.

"Come ahead on, now!" Papa hollered everybody up one cold November morning in 1941. It was a special day – hog killing day! I almost peed myself with excitement. All the Stewart family would gather to share the day and perform in the ritual of preparing our meat for another year.

I swallowed about four biscuits with molasses and burst out the back door with Billy Ray:

BILLY RAY

They won't let me have my own knife ... nebber ... nebber one, single, killin' day do I ebber git my own sharp knife. Yeah, and you're too puny and sickly no how, but I kin bear down and take a hold wif a killin' knife. Let's go – come on Little Dunnud – we'll watch 'em light the fires under the boiling vats ... I'll race you. Huddee! I'm the fastest runner in this whole danged county!

The hogs were herded across the dirt road by me and Billy Ray. They went right into the pen because a trough was filled with corn cobs, special grain, and real rank garbage from several homes. My molasses gagged its way Northward..... whew!

As patriarch, Papa was presented with Uncle Kirky's best rifle. He chambered a round and yelled, "Are the vats a'boilin' proper? ... Alright, then I'll commence." And Papa shot four hogs right behind their left ears.

BILLY RAY

Huddee ... oh, Lord, Huddee! I got to git me a knife. I kin chop 'em and cut 'em deep and git a heap!

Papa boomed, "Quit that pullin' at your overalls, Billy, and be still now! Son, fetch me my knife a'stickin' in yonder fence post." And I made a bit of pee in my Long Johns as I carried Papa the knife like the Holy Grail. Then, with me right by his side, he methodically slit the throat of each hog – so deeply that blood spewed forth, changing the back yard into red mud. Billy Ray caught some spurts and rubbed his overalls ruby red:

BILLY RAY

You'll all see ... Huddee! Someday I could make the blood fly to the sky – someday I'll git her done too ... it'll rain blood on all of y'all.

The hogs were then dropped into the boiling vats and scraped of hair and grime until they were radiantly pink. All the colors and their changes held me spellbound. And then it hits me:

DONALD

I'd seen them, all four, at birth and now they looked the same except about three hundred pounds heavier. I looked at Papa and he put his hands on my shoulder ... Lord, I'm sure glad I didn't name them this year. It's always harder when you name the things you grow up with ... they're just like big, fat babies again ... yeah, and I know..... I know we had to kill them, and yeah, I'm sure I'll understand someday ... yeah, right.

Then Papa held me in his arms and hushed all assembled there as he raised his large knife:

PAPA

Lord God Almighty! We give thanks for this here abundance, and we know without you we are nothing. Bless this meat for the nourishment of bodies and give us your divine strength in all that we do – and, as always, we give you the glory! Can we get an Amen? ... Amen.

Papa approached the hogs who were hanging by their pierced hind legs – all stretched taut to bursting. And then he slit the hogs open from throat to ass and an explosion of innards and organs gushed forth into the waiting tubs. "Oooohwee!" keened the women folk.

Everyone went to his or her specialty of carving, cleaning, and sculpting meat. Now ... have you ever heard the phrase: "To gag a maggot"? That's what boiling hogs' intestines to make <u>chitlins</u> does to any human being more sensitive than a petrified rock. And ... I did lose some lunch later in the day of abundance, thanksgiving, and the union of our family.

DONALD

It was Saturday, December 6, 1941 – a day that still haunts my nights. I wanted to play but the wash tub was all full right after breakfast. So I was severely clean before Papa finished his chores. And then, Momma brought forth a new Sunday suit..... but this was Saturday. No matter, Papa's Papa had died and we would attend his funeral down the road in Dunn. The suit was a masterpiece of soft material – almost like velvet – and it had a feminine, frilly collar to go with it. "No ma'am," I won't wear that sissy suit! Whack! No, I won't wear such a thing either. Wham! My head spun sharply. No! I won't put it on, not ever. Snap!

Whack! And my own belt stung me unmercifully now. Momma, quit you killin' me ... I can't wear that thing ... quit! Momma ... Momma, no ... please, no more ... I wish I had died on you ... no! Ma ... Ma ... Mamma ... I ... I'm ah ... go ... gonna ... ah ... ah ... please ... I'll wear it ... ah ... ah will if you only ... please ... ah, ah ... can't catch any air ...

Daddy finally found me sitting still in the parlor and wanted to know if I had gotten soap in my eyes. Well, I was so "special" in Momma's beautiful handiwork, that I was declared a "handsome angel boy" by all there – except I knew inside that the stutter that erupted in me by way of my own belt's stinging blows might be more than a one-time thing.

And so ... we all drove to Dunn for the big family funeral. Even Billy Ray was dragged along in brand new overalls and a red hunter's cap:

BILLY RAY

I kin bear down and plough all confounded day ... if'en ... if'en ya'll would let me ... even on Sattadays like this 'un. I won't hush, Mabel ... now, hits 'pose to rain all next week and ... well, the aggerbaitin wevverman says he'll make it rain on the radio ... and then it's jist sit on the porch and count cars and shell peas and such. No ... y'all hush your mawfs, and Sister Teeney better keep aweay from me 'cause she's plum crazy and loves these here funerals ... when old dog Trixie was kilt by that uggy, yeller school bus ... we just put her in a hole by the vegetable garden ... so why do we have to make such a fuss over that old, mean-faced, fat man who was the biggest, lazy-assed bone I ebber seen!?!

With my belly still jumping and my throat raw, Billy Ray made perfect sense to me. Now ... Great-Grandpa Walker Haigwood Stevenson weighed about three hundred pounds and there he was, laid out in a special, handmade casket under the biggest pecan tree in the world. There was tons of food and talk of war and crops and car wrecks and such. Aunt Teeney twitched her way toward me and asked loudly: "My ... my, where did you get those beautiful, brown eyes?" And I jerked away and let her have it: "They came with my face!" Many men applauded me and Teeney twitched fiercely and ticked and twisted her way off to drive Preacher Johnson crazy for a while. He escaped her advances by lifting up a prayer of praise for one dead Walker Stewart. My Daddy pulled me away beside the porch and:

DADDY

> Now ... I wonder, Son, how come that man can be such a marvel of Christian charity and the best father in the world when he had five children of his own and 'bout *eight* others of ev'ry stripe and color hereabouts? And I never once seen him outta that great chair of his. Yeah ... that's some trick doing all that Christian work and farm-bossin' and child-making and never get up off your blubbery ass. And it puzzles me powerfully to ever wonder how all his good women got to making all them "rainbow of babies" from the high throne of that mighty chair. Just think of the trick of that, Son.

And as I was trying to fathom my Daddy's words and the images that ran through my confused brain, I was suddenly snatched away to the Preacher's little platform by my Momma. Lord, God! I, the only great-grandchild and her "beloved one from God," would honor the dearly departed and all assembled there with a hymn. My throat became raw cotton and my belly heaved in and out like my first breath on earth. The only hymn I cared about finally found its way upward and out through my dry, chapped lips:

DONALD

Amazing grace, how sweet the sound, that saved a wretch like me. I once was lost, but now I'm found – was blind but now I see.

When we've been there, ten thousand years – bright shining as the Son. We've no less days to sing God's praise, than when we first begun.

Then Daddy's hands were there as the big tree started to spin and, just before darkness came over me, I heard them at it again: Momma said, "It's good for my son to get up in public and show his God-given talents. And don't you interfere – you're not even here most of the time." Then Daddy snapped back, "Well, Mabel, maybe there *is* God up there if he allows me that!"

I wish I could forget the next few moments, but so it goes … Momma announced: "And a little child shall lead them!" And she marched me right up to the open casket and held me over my great-grandfather…. "Kiss this beloved brother of Jesus goodbye." I felt burning bile in my throat and, when my lips were pressed against his smelly, yellow cheek, the taste of "human wax" hit my mouth, and swirling black rings hit my head, and then gushing vomit hit my "previous special Sunday suit." It seemed like hours before I was conscious of Billy Ray:

BILLY RAY

Here, Dunnud, eat some of this here chockee cake – it's plum full of busted-up pecans and this sweet milk is reaaal cold. You sung flatout purdy up there, but that kissin' mess was uggy of your Momma Mabel … and y'all hear me good, Sister Teeney, don't you ever try to mess with Dunnud now. Hush your mawf and ebberbody! Y'all listen to me now ... this cake is good enough for some more and I'm a'gonna steal me a bit Pepsi from Sommers and all y'all leave Little Dunnud alone, 'cause if Teeney or Mabel says one more aggerbaitin' word today, I'm ... I'm gonna slap the dog shit slam outta both of 'dem. Now ... say Amen to that, Preacher man.

The ride home was in silence except for Daddy patting my knee too hard when the giggles would hit him.

After breakfast on Sunday, I was sitting on Papa's lap listening to the Good Time Gospel Hour. His coffee was steaming and he fired up a Lucky Strike from the green-labeled pack, and I swear I started smoking because of the rich, aromatic, and soothing experience of Papa's deep inhaling and the perfect smoke rings from his exhale. Then crackle ... hiss ... hiss ... crackle! Beep, beep ... beep ... the radio broke up right in the middle of "I've got a home in glory land that outshines the sun." ... "Ladies and gentlemen, the President of the United States" ... Mr. Roosevelt spoke eloquently and, as we all know, there was a day then that has lived in infamy – December 7, 1941 ... and even Daddy went to church that Sunday, and I discovered that he sang like an angel.

Later in the day Daddy was excited:

DADDY

For once I say, "Praise God!" I'm gonna be the first one in line, by Christ. Who the hell do these infernal, slant-eyed, yeller migets think they're messin' with? No one gives a continental damn about my education now. I can have a whole airfield wired up in one flat day and keep a carbine ready to do its work on any of Hitler's or Tojo's boys. Give me a choice, and I'd rather take on the yeller plague! Kill 'em all save six –

Uncle Kirky hushed everybody by just scooping me up off Papa's lap and moving to the big bay windows and I felt his belly moving in and out like mind did at birth ... Papa's brother, the injured hero of World War I, was silently crying inside:

UNCLE KIRKY

Hush your loud mouth, Freeman, and hold your own son for once. Well ... here we go with the damned English again. Be still now Billy ... hey, boys now all y'all just be easy now – there'll always be enough wars to go around – that's for damned sure. We haven't learned a danged thing since men lived in caves and stumbled on to fire ... and believe it, this time there'll be a precious plenty of fire to go around. It won't matter, Freeman, whether you fly a plane, work a ship, or land with the Marines ... 'cause the fire and the pain and the death keep coming ... if you ever prayed in your life, ol' son, now's the time to plead with the Man up there to keep our allies going ... going strong. We all got to bear down and take a holt now. There now ... Billy Ray stop pulling at yourself and, Donald, me and your Papa need us some good helpers here ... got some real jobs of work now. Stay close and learn, ol' son, 'cause we're gonna need new mules by the time we wear ol' Clyde slam out.

What a team Billy Ray and I made. Well water in a bucket on a rope ... corn shucking ... hog slopping ... weed chopping ... chicken feeding ... on and on and finally, I was even able to drive old, gentle Clyde and bring a tobacco drag in from the hot, humid fields.

World War II was a wonderful time for kids. You felt a sense of union and safety on the farm. Even the rationing and saving and being ever appreciative of every comfort you had gave a sense of centered purpose. You felt you were part of something very powerful and important. The only thing that confused me mightily was when Papa said "that getting in this war was the best thing that could have happened to America – since we had barely limped out of the Great Depression." And I remember saying to myself, "Yeah, and I'll bet I'll understand that someday too."

Papa read about a ship in the Battle of Midway where men were walking in corridors ankle deep in the blood of their comrades. And my Daddy, who had come home from Camp Gordon, Georgia, where he was an electrician for Army housing, flung his newspaper to the floor:

DADDY

The only blood I'll be walkin' in will be at hog killin' time or such. Hell ... I know I'm needed here to work and maintain the supplies, but that don't get her done for me. I'll do my part, but it pains me pretty deep to miss the Big Show. What hurts the most is that even the damned Sea Bees turned me down. The doctors couldn't get a cigarette paper to slide under these slapdab, flat-assed feet of mine. I swear 'fore God I'd had just as soon stayed on the top floor of that burning building up in Raleigh as lose out on soldiering. Who knew I'd land in a pile of bricks when I jumped to safety ... some kind of joke eh, Old Man up there! I musta set the world's record for broken arches that cold day. Well ... my jobs here ain't no joke 'cause I'm one rank, hard-assed worker and if it's broke, I can fix it, and if it's new-fangled, I can learn to make the circuits hum and sing. Y'all go ahead now – kill 'em for me and show me some medals, boys. Bring me a souvenir ... one of them

Jap swords would do just fine. For now, Little Bunk, bring your Daddy some ice for the J.T.S. Brown Sour Mash bourbon here. I'll be just fine here on the home front 'cause they ain't going to ration the bourbon ... hell, that would be plumb un-American right now.

Daddy scared me that day, but even so, I wanted to be as close to him as I could – even after I heard Uncle Kirky tell Papa that my Daddy was driving a stake through his own heart and manhood and that whiskey was no way to play the cards you're dealt.

Well, we joined Daddy in Camp Gordon, Georgia – lived in one bed room with my little bed pushed under theirs during the day. Everything was in short supply, but I was in heaven watching the trains come and go and soldiers waving and throwing occasional nickels to me when I saluted them. Across the tracks was "colored town," and one day, I motioned for this Negro boy to come on and play with me on my Red Flyer wagon. He motioned that he better not, but I waved him on and my one true friend there became Little Lucas Jackson. All I had ever heard or seen back on the farm was that black people were "lazy-assed Niggers and a necessary burden." But Daddy always had a piece of candy or gum for Little Lucas every time he had one for me and teased us unmercifully about getting *pickaninnies* in our hair. We'd check each other's hair every day to see if the mysterious monsters had materialized.

Momma was obsessed that I would catch head lice or worse from Lucas whom she called, "That nice little *nigra* boy." Daddy yelled out of the bathroom one day: "God damn it, Mabel, quit the bullshit. Either call them Negroes or Niggers, but cut the Nigra crap!"

Things got worse between them and back to Papa's farm we went when Daddy took off for Portsmouth, Virginia and the Naval Shipyards. All during the long, crowded bus ride to North

Carolina – sometimes having to sit on a soldier's lap for hundreds of miles – I kept thinking about Little Luke and the field hands I would see working again. Damn! I was confused ... still am. Why do folks have such a powerful need to be superior to those who are somehow different? And I heard the refrain in my head again ... "You'll know someday ... someday, you'll understand."

Maybe I would know some things soon because, after only one week, I came home and announced at supper that I *loved* school – even if my teacher was sixty-five and what Daddy would have called "pruned-faced." I loved her attention and the promise that if I kept working hard I could lead the rhythm band come Christmas, 1942. Well ... some straight "A's." later and I had a baton and the most beautiful red and white uniform I had ever seen—

DONALD

Lord ... I was teased terribly about being teacher's pet and all. I said "Too bad, I'm the leader" as I set my cap and fix my chinstrap. I almost nicked a finger on the severe crease in my starched white pants and, just before I made my "entrance" on the auditorium stage, I thought of Little Luke in Georgia. He did the best "hambone-ing" in the world ... "hambone, hambone, where you been ... 'round the world and going again" – I sure could have used his talent among all the rachets, triangles, drums, and kazoos. But there I was ... a red-capped speck among a sea of white faces. It was strange because I wasn't nervous and I thought – it's Christmas and I wonder if Luke has a Christmas program going on with a black Baby Jesus? Anyway ... I raised my baton and launched my "show business career" with a roaring rendition of "Red River Valley." The great applause made me feel ten feet tall and snap! I saluted the audience. The applause came with some whistles then, and Preacher Johnson exclaimed, "God Bless America!" In honor of the birthday of Jesus, our finale was sung. All us little people harmonized and gave praise in a joyful noise with "Away in a Manger," some mothers cried and dabbed their eyes, and I caught my Uncle Horace, home on leave, reach for his Army handkerchief. Tears came in my eyes too because I was *somebody*! A performer! And I had a uniform too and led "my troops." I took a solo bow, and then, as I backed up, I raised my arms to lead a company bow and zing ... snap! My infernal belt broke loose and my perfect white pants hit my glimmering shoe tops. All "my troops" giggled low then pointed at my underwear, and one boy started a refrain of "flower sack drawers ... flower sack drawers." Struggling to pull my pants up, my tears of joy turned to scalding tears of horror and failure. And I remembered what Momma had said at the funeral just before I kissed a dead man's cheek: "And a little child shall lead them."

Suddenly, out of nowhere, Uncle Horace was there – scooping me up in his strong arms and my tears wet down his chestful of medals. He carried me to his '39 Ford as he pushed everybody out of our way. Suddenly I was somehow on his lap and, as we pulled out, he said, "Here you drive ... take the wheel boy and I'll do the gears and pedals." I said I could only try ... and that I guessed I could never go back to school again.

UNCLE HORACE

Shoot fire boy! You'll go back – go back and lead "your troops" just like me when my leg heals some better. Hell, boy ... you'll heal too. Just remember goin' *back* again is harder than goin' in the first place. The first time you don't know how rough things can get – you just go ahead on. But goin' back *again* when you are the most scared ... that's the hard part. Remember that now, in life, war, whatever ... you show them that you can keep on a' keepin' on ... fear and all. Hell, son, that's what *I* got to do – you know, use *my* fear as fuel just like gas makes this car go. You were brave up there tonight ... don't let a little accident take that from you. Never mind now and ... Hey, watch out for that patch of ice.

Back at Papa's farmhouse, there was a little party with ham, biscuits, cake and pie, and Aunt Teeney tried to sing Christmas carols as she pounded the piano into submission. In a lull, at one point, Billy Ray got the Christmas spirit:

BILLY RAY

Huddee! I a'gonna git my sharp, kinlin' hatchet and chop up the whole danged piano if Teeney don't stop a killin' the purdy music ... nothin' but an aggerbaitin' mess of noise 'round here. Little Dunnud kin' sing if he wants to ... but I say that Sister Teeney ought to be in the Army – like ... like a hospital nurse or such so the little yeller-midget Japs could take a holt of her and ... yeah, they could do her uggy like that! Sure ... y'all are all quiet now, I reckon. Go ahead on outta this room right now. I like this purdy fire and the tree a'smellin', but that confounded, lazy-assed sister is the one ... she ate the last piece of chockee pie ... so there, all of y'all ... I hate Christmas.

Then Uncle Horace and I were alone in the big rocking chair by the fireplace. He talked about having to go back in one short week and how he'd have to train new troops at Fort Bragg. His voice got low and hoarse when he mentioned how the cold hurt his busted-up knee. Still feeling sick about my performance debut, I threw my traitorous belt in the fireplace and "damned it to burn in hell just like Hitler would."

Then Uncle Horace lit up a Chesterfield and I breathed deeply and asked if I could have a drag.

UNCLE HORACE

No ... no siree-bob, Little Captain of the Band, but you can go rummage under that Christmas tree for a 'wee' box from me. Don't you worry about your Momma now ... there ... open it up and see now ... there's a man-sized belt for a good soldier, but I'll be damned there's no buckle for it. J.C. Penney can't keep good help anymore ... let me see now ... yep, there something in my shirt pocket here. Well ... you can close your mouth anytime now ... it's yours ... all yours, just clamp that buckle on – I've done cut the belt down to fit a 'wee' fellow. Now ... see if all others don't look up to you at school now. Their teasing and talk will hush just like I hushed the Kraut Lieutenant when he reached for my hand to shake it as I handed him a Hershey bar. Seemed like the young Nazi wanted to be friends when I captured him but ... but ... well, we were both wore slam out and freezing, but he seemed calm and kinda gentle. So ... I eased up and gave him some water while we waited for a jeep driver to find us. Hell, boy, we even showed each other pictures of our wives. Then, as I heard a jeep a'streamin' through the ice and snow, he kinda *acted* out like being hungry. So ... I scroughed in my sack and found a mashed-up chocolate bar ... he smiled and reached for it with his left hand and I smiled as he tore the wrapper with his teeth and his right hand kinda twitched toward his boot, and as he chewed on the chocolate, I shot him right between the eyes with my '45. You see, right inside his boot was an ice pick with a purdy silver handle ... kinda matched his fancy belt buckle you got there. You see ... I knew by his eyes ... watch people's eyes ... they perform ... they act out ... say one thing and mean another, but the eyes hold the truth of things. In the picture shows it's safe to "act out" but not in life. It ain't safe nowhere, ol' son ... so watch people and listen for what's under the words you hear. Maybe you'd like to be a soldier someday ... or be up on the stage performing even if your britches did fall down. You've got years to choose in, but please enjoy your schoolin' and don't wind up ignorant like me. Yes ... it's true, you hear me now ... you watch, you listen for the truth and you'll find your own way, but don't get fooled about your journeys being safe ... no man's safe except alone with a fine dog that loves him, but that's about as good as it gets.

And as the tears came to his eyes, Horace looked into the fire and rubbed his shot-up leg. I thought about my Daddy, far away in the shipyards, and whispered to myself, "yeah, I will know things some day and Merry Christmas men, far and near ... it may not be safe ... but it's still Christmas."

Then it was school, chores, junior choir practices and busy adventures with Billy Ray. Then, near Good Friday, 1943, a car pulled up at Papa's and, slam-bam, there stood my Daddy. He's bussed in from Virginia to Raleigh then thumbed on home. He looked awful tired from pulling double shifts and working holidays for extra money.

Daddy set me down inside and got a dipper of water in the kitchen. As he tried to hug Momma, she held her head up for a kiss, but when the bourbon breath hit her she pulled away and got busy churning butter. I found a box of twenty-four Hersheys in his duffle bag and I didn't even bother to ask how he smuggled them out of the shipyard. Daddy just winked and did a "thumbs up." Then my hand hit a couple of bourbon bottles and my face dropped some, but I was surely lifted up again when my hand drew out a gleaming, silver '45 automatic pistol. Daddy then stuck it in my new belt and declared I now had something to go with my valuable Nazi belt buckle. A machinist friend of his had made this perfect replica, and later Daddy carved a wooden rifle for Billy Ray. As I was practicing a quick draw, my Momma's hand was on my shoulder, and I was instructed not to tease with my gun and to be careful ... always remembering, she said, "The Bible says be ye not proud ... be ye not puffed-up." I didn't understand the Bible's commandment about pride and even Baby Jesus would know that, as skinny as I was, I could never be "puffed-up."

We carried our "weapons" with us everywhere. Papa's farm became one international battlefield. Cows, hogs, chickens, and even trusted hound dogs were chased, captured, or shot down where they stood. Jap and German troops were all around us and our guns blazed away. Pine cones were our hand grenades and they rained death on our enemies from our secret headquarters in Papa's barn. We were safe there ... that is until Billy Ray got too excited while shooting out of the left windows and elbowed me right into mid-air. The first of me to hit the planked floor were my shoulder blades, and that cold, empty feeling of my first moment on earth came back ... darkness and no air to breathe ... I was hung up between life and death ... and the world was void ... again:

BILLY RAY (crying)

Oh ... Huddee! Dunnud, Huddee! Don't die on me. It were the nasty Germans that hit you ... they were all around here ... they near 'bout burnt down our smokehouse yonder. They're a'comin' from all over ... ridin' on lazy-bone tractors and ... and hep me, Lordee, hep me ... stay with me, Dunnud!

... Then as Billy Ray lifted me up, he squeezed by stomach so hard that my temples almost exploded with the rush of air to my brain. With lungs on fire, once again my scream of life brought my Daddy's gentle hands and soothing, whiskey voice:

DADDY (kneeling)

There, ol' son ... there you be now. Just be still a minute. Well ... "Little Sergeant," looks like you ain't gonna get no R & R from this patrol ... no sir, there's nothing broke, but you do need to get your breathing back to normal. Let's see now ... here we go. This little old paper sack don't need to house all these ten-penny nails ... now ... now, you just breathe slow into this bag for a 'wee' bit. There ... there you go ... easy, ol' son, easy goes it. Now, the mess cook's in the command post kitchen yonder order y'all to wash up for your dinner. This mid-day we're having fried chicken, black-eyed peas, turnip salad, and green apple turnovers. Come on men, let's fall in.

During our dinner, Daddy announced that he was going back to Virginia to work more, long overtime hours – saving for our own house. Papa and Two-Mammas agreed that my schooling would be better served in a bigger town. My back and stomach stopped hurting when I thought of seeing the big ships, and maybe even getting to go to work with my Daddy someday.

The days now passed routinely ... but Billy Ray and I were given strict orders to behave quietly in the house. And I couldn't figure out why Momma got sick to her stomach before breakfast all the time. Finally, riding in his car one day, Papa broke one of his long silences.

PAPA

You see now ... you see, it's like this here. When y'all move on up to Virginia, you'll be taken along another passenger, you know. Yes ... son, it's true, your Momma is ... well, she's better now and it looks like she'll make it on through fine this time. Well, yes, there you be ... you're gonna be a big brother purdy soon, and I know you'll be a good 'un ... strong and true and a help and a comfort. There, you been tolt, so you commence right now by helpin' your Momma out all you can. There's a good ol' man ... and ... well, I'll miss you, son, when you move on North ... cause ... well, you know ... you'll know, you'll know ... someday.

When Papa pulled into the yard, I leaped out and ran in circles yelling and whistling. Billy Ray joined me, not even asking me why we were rolling in the red clay of the ditch out front. Then Two-Mamas told us to be quiet or she'd find a good stinging use for her sturdy yard broom. Besides, she said, I could yell "Baby Brother" all I wanted, but they were praying for a baby girl ... a pink and white baby girl and thank you, Jesus. Then she sang:

"Laura Lee, Laura Lee, Sunshine in your hair ...
Lord, oh Lord, we're thanking Thee for our Laura Lee."

Then it hit me like lightning ... oh, Lord have mercy, a sister!?! What in blue blazes was a guy to do with a sister!?! And, as I chucked a rock at the chickens, I exclaimed: "Shit, a sister! It ain't fair!" Mother must have had that new-fangled radar Daddy told us about because up went her bedroom window and she hollered: "Donald Max Stewart, you get you and your nasty mouth in here right this minute." As I walked to the kitchen door, I wondered why is it your Momma always calls out your whole, blasted name, for all the world to hear, when you're in serious trouble? ...

In the farm lands, school got out in mid-May so the kids could help tend the tobacco crops. Billy Ray and I got to do the best job in the world to us – we got to de-worm the tobacco stalks. No sprays anywhere – the crops were worked by hand.

Now ... tobacco worms are a slimy green and can get as big as a man's thumb. You just pulled them off the sticky leaves and smashed them on the ground, and their green juice oozed into nightmarish patterns in the rich earth ... then one day I stopped in my row of work and looked back at Billy Ray:

BILLY RAY

> Lookee here now, you cain't even know why I brung this here wheelbarrow ... Well, it's ... it's 'cause it's time ... time I done it. Now, you no-account lazy-ass, come on, chunk your'n in this barrow with mine. It's their time ... I been studying on it and it's time for 'em to die. Come on Dunnud, chunk 'em all ... that's it, git her done now. Hot hell fire! Here's one fatter than my blistered big toe!

And so we toiled and laughed and triumphantly wheeled our "prisoners" back to the house and set up "headquarters" under Two-Mama's beautiful chinaberry tree. Billy Ray told me to keep watch and disappeared. I teased a tobacco worm with a twig and felt very powerful, and suddenly, out of nowhere, Billy Ray's strangely, smiling face was glaring at me:

BILLY RAY

> Here ... her's yourn. There's two purdy, red bricks and here's *your* own hammer. I'm gonna work with this here ballpene one 'cause it's spankin'

new. I'm mighty right about this job of work, Little Dunnud. I been studying on it and a'dreaming about it and ... well, it's time to do it now. So, here's your Pepsi and I got us a whole gunny sack of peanuts I been cravin' for. We won't get too full of just puny peanuts 'fore suppertime ... listen now, I seen it all last night ... it's the war and we can't get to kill any of them squinty-eyed, yeller midget Japs, but these here, green 'bacca worms are my best enemy-like. Papa said they had to die for hurtin' our crops and Uncle Kirky even said it was like an invasion and damn 'em to hell! They're gonna die for it! Just like on the Jap island places these captured worms have done us an invasion and they live no more when I take a'holt. So, come on now, brick 'em and bust 'em hard to Hell for the invasion they done us.

And so ... we revenged the green worm "invasion" of our farm. Hammers crashed on the bricks, and fat worms exploded sending green life juices oozing out all over freshly cut grass and prim flower beds. Then I almost exploded when Two-Mama's yard broom hit the back of my head. More blows rained on me because every time I tried to get up I would slip and slide in the slimy, slick juice I had hammed out. Billy Ray ran out back and disappeared in the tall cornfield. Of course, it was all my fault, and it was my Daddy in me that caused "such behavior of a devil." Even though I spoke of Billy Ray's plan and execution, it was no good. I was ordered to pray for our souls and especially for Billy because he was "our Christian cross to bear."

Months later, all was cleansed again because it had just rained and the red clay road was a paradise for a barefoot boy. Then it came! Papa shouted from his black '39 Ford: "It's a boy! God has sent us another man child!" Of course, I ran in circles and Billy Ray followed me pulling at his crotch. I just kept chanting, "Brother, Brother, Brother, oh Buddy, Brother of mine!"

In her sterile hospital room it was quiet ... yeah, too quiet. Momma wouldn't even name the baby. She was hysterical, one: because it was a boy and two: he had reddish sprigs of hair and real slanty eyes. The topper came when a big, fat nurse wrote out my Daddy and Momma's whole names on a pad and, doing a combination, my brother was finally given a legal birth certificate as one: Ellis Lee Stewart. Mother flung the pink baby dress she had made across the room and shouted: "I can't stand this. I just can't have it now! It's got Jap eyes and there's no red hair in my family. It's your Daddy again, and God's working on my sins and look at the mess we're in with the Japs and just go look in that blue blanket in there!"

I did and my brother squeezed my fingers with a strong grip and when he smiled at me he was just, plain perfect ... except the problem was ... Daddy wasn't there again.

... A new life in our midst and a new home of our own – for the first time. Alexander Park was a war-time housing project outside Portsmouth, Virginia. The rich tidewater dirt provided our streets, and a huge wooded area across from our tiny, four-room, brown-boarded house gave us kids a marvelous playground—especially for war games. All the homes were identical and you had to keep your bearings or you might get irrevocably lost in the maze of what seemed like "brown boxes."

I was scared a lot but anything new is scary. People had moved from all over the country, and all the different accents and attitudes fascinated me. But at night, I especially yearned for the warm safety of the farm and even the strange, but special, companionship of Billy Ray. No matter ... forget the familiar and the safe – it was war time and we all had to be brave in our own way.

DONALD

It was almost Labor Day ... time for excitement again because I lived for the challenges that school brought. I had new, flour-sack shirts, and Momma made me a glorious, corduroy jacket, with three pockets to hold my treasured mix of marbles—a passionate activity in our neighborhood. We also played "war" and I got "killed" a lot because I had the German belt buckle, and my '45 had to become my enemy Luger. Finally ... it came and the school yard was swarming with all manner of kids named Kravitz, DiVita, and even a Waxmunski ... but, of course, no blacks. First assemely we were warned never to go near the Negro housing project called Tuxton. And I thought of Luke in Georgia again and wanted to ask the forbidden question that plagued me at Papa's farm and, now here: Why are children separated just because of the color of their skin? Yeah", I thought, "maybe I will know someday ... but know what? ... " Now, I loved the smell of new textbooks and soon I brought home my first report card. Daddy held me on his lap and read it for the longest time ... mumbling occasionally about how he could have been a doctor and all with a proper education. I always agreed with him, but felt sad because his bourbon breath and sweaty, khaki shirt, reeked of self-pity. He gave me a quarter and kissed my forehead and all my bad feelings left because, at last, we were all together in our own home ... then Mother grabbed my report card and read: "A" ... "A" ... "A" ... "A" ... good deportment and so on and then ah ... Lord! A "B" in handwriting! That would be remedied immediately because *she* had learned to pull her left hand around straight and so would I. Apply myself! Yeah, right, I will ... yes, we are judged in this world by the character of our handwriting as well as our appearance. I stopped the ruination of my joy at school by telling her that the coal bucket was empty and I would fill it from the bin out back. As I shoveled the black chunks of coal, I said out loud: "Why do I feel like Momma's got one arm and Daddy the other and they are pulling me apart like a wishbone at Thanksgiving dinner?" And a voice rang in my head with: "Don't you know that kids are play toys for grownups? Just keep shoveling – son."

I was working and playing hard and even got to decorate a big bulletin board at school urging all families to "Buy U.S. War Bonds!" My left-handed art work drew praise all around, and then, suddenly, my passion was shot down ... cruelly, my *bedroom* became my *school room* because, one after another, *"my enemy invaders" struck!* With only scattered weeks of relief, them came in waves: First, German measles, then the red measles ... followed by a messy tonsil and adenoids operation which precipitated a serious hemorrhaging and passing out cold in a pool of blood in the bathroom ... finally, a "truce" was called for a while, and I was back in school keeping my spirits and grades high and then I really had something to worry about: *Scarlet Fever*! And in pristine logic, Momma decided we had better change doctors since her food, care, handwriting practice, and fervent prayers had not helped so far:

DONALD

So ... sports fans, now my little all-American home was truly "invaded" by the Germans. Through my fevered brain, it seemed like I was in some Nazi war movie. There he was, in my own bedroom, leering through little round glasses. One Dr. Hugo Hess sent cold shivers to my heart, and again, my stomach churned and jumped for life as he said: "yah ... vee have seen this before ... the fever is much too high, and his weakness from the other illnesses is very problematic at this time." I felt like he might use electrical shock any minute as I lay between consciousness and oblivion. All I remember is: soup, crackers, ginger ale, comic books, hazy radio serials and, of course, turning putrid yellow from massive doses of the "Nazi" Dr. Hess' favorite innovation in my case – sulfur drug! I had to fight to live again! And fight I did! ... Finally, the fevered haze cleared, and I was going to make my first trip to the bathroom by myself. I must have looked like a newborn pony struggling to stay upright. ... N.G. ... No good. I fell flat-ass out. And split my head on the door jam. Momma got hysterical and her prayers soared skyward. Daddy was there for me again and gently and patiently helped me learn to walk again ... I remember thinking, with each awkward step: "My brain is still fried and Dr. Hess, you Nazi bastard, you got me didn't you? Try more sulfur torture – go one – try your muscle shocks – try your damnedest because, in the end, we tough-assed Americans will whip you evil sons-a-bitches!" Daddy loved my fevered outbursts but, of course, there was another terrible fight over my using cuss words. As the verbal bashings went on, I remembered a phrase Papa had used on the farm – "oil and water don't mix." Bracing with the back of a chair, I finally let loose: oil and water ... oil and water ... why are y'all still together? I can't be Momma's boy one minute and then be Daddy's boy and hate Sunday school like him ... Damn all Nazis who turn little guys like me yellow and weak ... I'm going back to school and work hard to be me ... just me ... and I am *not* what's wrong around here with you. Fight! ... fight all you want – go back to North Carolina, Momma. Daddy, go ahead on the road again ... or ... just ... just please stop using me to get at each other! And you both should know that baby brother Lee hears and feels all this mess too. So keep on hurting us all! Go ahead ... this little brown box of a house is a good battleground too ... we're still at war, you know!

... And just before my frenzy brought me flat to the couch, I heard them say ... "Freeman, he didn't mean it – it was just the medicine and his brain being fevered too long ... he's still my shining star."

... I don't know, Mabel ... I read in a medical book once that when the brain gets fried too long, it's impossible for a body not to tell the truth."

And just before total blackness covered me on the couch – I thought: "Hey God, can I just skip a few years and go ahead on and be eighteen right now?" And then a "picture" in my head that looked like Dr. Hess answered: "No, Little Man, you must serve your time."

By the time I was back in school and getting stronger, we were well into 1944. Relatives were coming to work and live near us, and Momma and her brother Ashley got in a terrible fight over some gas coupons he had saved for a trip back to North Carolina. By Christmas, I personally understood rationing for real when my gun and holster set fell apart within a week. It was black and silver – all fancy like Roy Rogers wore, and I fought back the tears when I realized it was nothing but a decorated, cardboard substitute.

Then it came to me that Uncle Horace and our brave men needed all the leather, metal, gas, wool, cotton, and chocolate bars. Good, I thought, plague take 'em! Kick the hell out of those damn Nazis and slant-eyed Japs! Kill one for me and throw your Hershey wrapper on his dead, cold face for me!

Now, we all know there are wars on a grand scale, but sometimes it's the supposed little ones that tear at us and hurt the worst!

DONALD

Wayne Boyles and I went to see the movies, "Marine Raiders" and "Gung Ho!:" – a double feature for fifteen cents. We came home and played out the action until we were properly sweaty and grimy, and then, leaving the woods, I was suddenly in the big ditch with a muddy ass. Wayne was laughing like a crazy thing and offered me my rifle butt to pull me out. He said I was too puny to play sports let alone ever be a soldier ... and then, a few yards more, and I was in the ditch again. This time I crawled out like I had wings and grabbed his ankle and tried to pull him to the ground. He laughed harder and I fought off the angry tears and instead I let fly with, "You stupid, mule-assed cracker! Just because you're so much bigger than me, you think you're funny. You can't even read out loud when the teacher calls on you. You're a big, freckled face frog and you'll always be too stupid ... and a real chickenshit ... chickenshit ... chickenshit!"

His blow to my stomach caused a bit of vomit and Wayne ran with my B-B gun. I tore out full speed and caught the dumb ox with a shoe-top tackle. My rifle flew in the air and I got it, but his next punch landed near my left ear. My vocal chords started to tear with blind, black rage, and I held my rifle like a baseball bat, and when Wayne's gaping face got a few feet away and he raised his rock-filled hand, I swung with all I had and the gun snapped like a twig over his knee ... "Die, you son-of-a-bitch ... Why Wayne ... why?" And all he could get out was, "Cause ... 'cause you're smart and the teacher favors you all the time ... and my Daddy says y'all are too uppity what with you a'singin' in church and ... I don't know what all."

... We just sat there, crying together – me in anger and confusion and Wayne in agonizing pain. All I wanted was to be able to fight it out equally with our fists ... but I was always too little and no one showed me anything ... except I got a whipping from Momma for being "un-Christian" and Wayne lied and became a "hero" by saying he was injured playing football with the big Catholic boys. As I cried myself to sleep, Daddy said Momma was wrong but what could a man do ... and, when he got the time, he'd teach me how to fight, but his slurred words produced no dreams of public victories and, like everything else so far, I knew that I'd have to learn things on my own ... and most probably the hard way.

In 1945 pictures started to come out in papers and magazines showing what the Nazis had done in some concentration camps in Poland and other places I was confused about. I had never known any Jews so far. We were mostly white protestants with a few Catholics thrown in and our teachers never discussed why the Jewish people were being singled out and eliminated. Momma told me that Jesus wasn't a "real Jew and to never confuse our Savior with one of them." I heard one neighbor man say that, "Hitler had done some bad things, but maybe some good could come out of this war if there were a few million less of them pushy, money-grubbing Kikes around!" I felt sick without knowing why and wanted my Daddy to tell me something to help me understand starving and gassing women and children, and the butchering of men just like a hog killing. But all my Daddy said as he passed our neighbor some bourbon was, "Screw them people ... screw'em all save six ... we never could trust those damned people anyway." Then I ... I just let loose again:

DONALD

I suppose I'll know about that someday ... someday I'll understand that, won't I ... yeah, someday shit! And I ran off in the dark ... running until I slumped in the grass by the big ditch. I stared into the ditch visualizing the stacked bodies in the magazine pictures. Later, I fell asleep wondering about the word "superior" that had been on our vocabulary test at school. I guess some people, whether on a playground or in Europe or Japan, just have to be above others and "persecute people ... persecute" ... I didn't even like looking it up in the dictionary ... somehow, I felt like I knew those kids in the striped "pajamas" staring out through the barbed wire with vacant eyes ... like a dying rabbit I came across walking in the woods one day. The bunny looked at me with wide, pleading eyes, and I put it to sleep with the butt of my Red Ryder rifle. The same one that broke Wayne Boyles' bullying knee. Lord, God a'mighty! Somebody talk to me! Because I'm one confused youn'un! And, before I slept, I thought of Little Luke down in Georgia and hoped that his black hide was safe and not causing the white people any trouble.

Read all about it! -- D-Day the sixth of June! Everybody pulling together ... Allies ... Normandy ... Omaha Beach ... Operation Overlord! Berlin, here we come! The war games in our woods escalated gloriously, and me and my Nazi belt buckle were usually on the run – as heroically as I could manage.

Then ... I got the chance to be a real hero. At Daddy's work, some small bolt had dropped off into an awkward section of a submarine engine and no tool could reach it. A very skinny arm and nimble fingers were desperately needed. Since Daddy was

"Big Stew," the top trouble-shooter, I was enlisted to be his "specialist."

After we were cleared by a Marine guard, I noticed how everyone seemed to respect my Daddy at his work. This surprised me because of his attitude and position at home with Momma. As the submarine came into view, I dismissed the question: Why would a man be one person at work and behave like someone else at home? ... Forget about it ... I have a man's job of work to do.

DONALD

I negotiated the sub's passageways just fine, but I'll never know how grown men do it. In the engine room, a fat man with about fifty tattoos saluted me with, "Come on, Little Stew, let's get her done" ... There was a tricky "L" section inside the engine where the bolt had drifted. Stripped down to my undershirt, and ready with Daddy's precise instructions – I was ready to win the war. It seemed to take forever to get my thin, greasy arm down to where the "L" turn was ... then my index finger felt it! I lay flat out and took a deep breath as Daddy held my belt and I made my right turn up to the elbow. Fishing in the grease ... probing ... fingering ... lower, Daddy, lower ... more and ... then, my middle finger touched the inch-and-a-half bolt ... wiggling down ... straining ... my shoulder joint on fire ... I had it! Thumb and middle finger ... pull out ... slowly ... easy ... then Daddy tried to help too much and my arm jerked toward my body as my knuckles hit the top of the "L" turn and my middle finger flexed and jumped and I said a quiet, "holy greasy Jesus!" And the bolt floated away deeper into the engine block. Frantic! And remembering Uncle Horace's earlier Christmas message: "Go back ... go back again when you're the most afraid – that's bravery!" I did ... I did ...

I tore my knuckles and blood and oil mixed, thick and sticky. Nothing worked and the bolt floated away too deep. Then the tears mixed in with the blood and oil and Daddy held me to his sweaty chest. The tattooed chief called for a first aid man and, after I got cleaned up, I got to eat supper with the sailors. Ham, lima beans, corn, and peach cobbler, and I felt a little better. Daddy's big contribution was explaining why the Navy served day-old bread, easy digestion and the prevention of bloating were evidently essential to worthy sea duty. The crew gave me a cap, a local medal, and six Milky Ways which made me feel even lower. Somehow Uncle Horace's spirit was with me, but then flashes of my pants falling down again hit me, but the big tattooed man held me up in the air and boomed: "We do our damned, dead-level best aboard this ship and that's what the little swabbie done ... that's all. He gave us his best and God Bless You. You're all-American in our book!" When the applause died ... It was like some fever broke and I was dizzy and kind of floaty.

I floated all the way home in the car listening to the radio report on "the Battle of the Bulge and how a lot of paratroopers were very trapped and cold." Daddy said he bet the 101-Airborne boys were taking the surrender leaflets the Nazis dropped and making good use of them in the outhouse. It kinda put my situation with the dropped, greasy bolt in perspective and I hoped the weather would clear up over some frozen, foggy place called Bastogne.

One Saturday night at the movies, Daddy finally admitted that "Singin' Sandy" – one John Wayne – really couldn't sing a lick and, right after I asked why Big John wasn't in the war, the newsreel came on. The images were everlasting up there on the screen. People were lined up crying in some quiet, powerful union over the death of President Franklin Delano Roosevelt. Black folks and white openly grieving together. No superiority or segregation were registered in the great loss – especially since victory seemed so close at hand. My Daddy practically worshipped Mr. Roosevelt, but then I got confused again because I overheard a teacher say that our late President was part Jew – that he just had to be. God! I thought, why would that matter? Then later, one rainy night, in a kinda twilight sleep, I prayed:

DONALD

Dear God, please help me to understand all these images in my mind and the different confusing words that keep pounding away: Whites, Negroes, Jews, Catholics, Rich Farmers, Field Hands, Two Different Water Fountains, and "Colored" Restrooms, and "Back of the Bus" … and hell – excuse me, God – President Roosevelt wasn't Jewish at all and Little Luke never got any "picaninnies" and, just before I asked Him if His son, Jesus, really did have light brown hair and blue eyes – sleep covered me and soon I was in a hellacious fight scene as John Wayne's Little Buckaroo Buddy … smashing bottles and chairs over the bad guys who looked like Nazis in cowboy hats … no "real" questions got answered but, deep, "play-like" sleep came and it was so sweet.

Routine set in now in 1945. The war machine here hummed like on automatic pilot. "Give 'em Hell" Harry S. Truman was President and Daddy liked him because, "he wouldn't take any crap off anybody." That sounded good, but made me sad too because Daddy sure took a lot of criticism and strain from Momma and he was drinking more as he complained about not being promoted in the shipyard. To which Momma would reply: "Come to church and pray with me about it. Give your soul to Jesus, and God will work in His wonderful ways." I thought, "Not now, Momma. Not now." Too late … and Daddy replied:

DADDY

Go to church with you!?! That'll be the damned day when you see a new star in the East and three more happy wisemen! I don't need any pinched-faced, weak-livered, sissy-assed, money-grubbing *liar* to help me out at my work. And, unless you want blood all over your fresh-polished linoleum, you'd better never ask your precious Preacher to come to this house again to pray for my sinful soul – not in the house I pay for. You talk about standing naked before God on the day of judgment ... mercy me, what an ugly sight that would be. If there is a God, he'd throw about 99% of all y'all back down to the fiery earth after he got a look at his handiwork. Look yonder at the calendar – it's Wednesday and there's a prayer meeting tonight, I'm sure. So ... please go pray that your Preacher – the Reverend Potter – hasn't skipped town with the Building Fund and I'll catch some peace and quiet here with my newspaper and Drew Pearson, and maybe hear some sane words from Edward R. Murrow. And that's my earnest prayer for tonight ... yes, Amen!

... And they still didn't get why I was always playing out movies in my room and reading and drawing ... pretending a lot seemed the healthy thing to do.

No need to play at being a Nazi any more because the Germans quit and surrendered on May 9, 1945. V-E Day! And I put my belt buckle away in a drawer with a gloriously victorious edition of Life Magazine. But now the Japanese would bend, but not break. And it got very confusing to me that suicide could be an honorable part of their culture and religion. You see, there was a Catholic boy named Dominic who told me he wanted to kill himself over his Daddy beating them all so fierce in drunken rages, but he feared something called hot, burning purgatory even more than having his Momma's teeth knocked out. Here we go again, I thought, the Japs can be welcomed in their heaven for jumping off a cliff and an Italian Catholic can't even think of getting relief from going hungry and having head lice. No, a good Catholic must endure or else. So ... I asked Momma about all of this and was told that *only Baptists* and *maybe* a few sprinklings of Methodists had a handle on getting into Heaven.

DONALD

Well ... I felt some pity and hoped that a whole bunch of Japs had made their peace because Colonel Paul Tibbetts, a man Daddy called "a good ol' boy" – flying the B-29 – "The Enola Gay," dropped something called an Atomic Bomb on a little place called Hiroshima and Daddy swung me around in celebration but then whispered to me: "Son, the world will never be the same." There were thousands of deaths and babies burned like French fries and the suicides didn't matter now because, Lord knows, the Japanese people didn't ask for any mushroom cloud to float up to their Heaven on ... but still, they wouldn't lay down and quit. So ... on August 9, 1945, Frederick Bock, in his plane called "Bock's Car," dropped another A-Bomb on Nagasaki ... yellow skin melted off like the hides off the hogs in the boiling vats on the special killin' day on Papa's farm ... and I thought: "Why the funny names for a flying fortress of horror and death ... and it came to me right clear – I may be little and just taking "baby steps" in this world, but Momma's version of God in Heaven was all wrong. He did have some kind of special sense of humor. He let us make a bomb that could fry whole islands and then give us a beautiful mushroom cloud for the souls to float up to His

Heaven on ... yes, sir. The Lord, God sure beats all ... doesn't he?

I felt queasy about not beating the Japanese, fair and square, just like when I had to use my rifle butt on Wayne Boyles to make him stop tormenting me. And, as usual, when I wanted to sit down and really talk about things, the grownups around me just caused more confusion.

DADDY (drinking)

Ol' Give 'Em Hell Harry done the right thing and probably saved about a half a million lives ... can you imagine our boys having to invade Japan? Lord, a'mercy now ... that good, Christian, puffed-up partridge of a Baptist neighbor of mine yonder – my wife's very favorite tenor in their wailing choir of a Sunday – now he thinks dropping the bomb was sinful and cowardly, that we could have ended this most righteous of wars with more human dignity ... yeah, you hypocritical bastards, there was whole bunches of dignity at Pearl Harbor and Bataan – just go ask General Wainwright ... .Are y'all sure you won't join me in a toast ... come on hoist up a jar of ol' J.T.S. Brown to us delivering the bomb ... come on now, we got her done, didn't we? ... Now, tell y'all what I'm gonna do ... I'm gonna get me a sweatshirt made up with letters on my chest that tell the truth about how we ended the war. Right or wrong, my ass. Yes, sir. Let my shirt tell the truth 'cause she's gonna read? EXCUSE ME, BUT YOU MUST HAVE ME CONFUSED WITH SOMEONE WHO GIVES A SHIT! Thank you, and that's my hymn for today.

Portsmouth, Virginia was one long, rousing party for days after V-J Day. All branches of servicemen blended into one victorious voice of relief and celebration ... whooping, drinking, kissing each other's wives and girlfriends. I was allowed to go downtown by myself for the first time to see the re-release of John Ford's classic, "Stagecoach."

When I stepped out of the theatre, another spontaneous street party erupted and I absolutely could not move. The bus stop was only three blocks away, but I was "imprisoned" in a mass of out-of-control winners! Panic hit ... victory is sweet but it too, like war, can scare a little guy to death. Finally, a chest full of medals was in my face, and a marine sergeant scooped me up on his wide shoulders and I could breathe again. His voice and confidence chased my fear away as:

BIG MARINE

Where to, Young Private? Oh ... yeah, I see the bus stop yonder. You're a brave one to come out on a night like this ... yeah, I thought the crazy partying was over too. Hey, you got your bus fare money? Here ... take this crisp dollar bill – I just run her off this morning so the ink may stain ya a bit. No ... no, now here, I can't eat another candy bar for months – so you take these two spare Hersheys. Here now, wipe that sweat off 'ya. Yes, sir, Little Soldier, I know all about wiping the old fear sweat. And hear me now ... I hate crowds too, and I don't intend to ever be cheek-to-ass hemmed in again – not on no ship, no landing craft, in no foxhole dug for two and holding five ... no, sir, your taste of panic back yonder is over for you and so's mine. I'm going back to Montana and live with the deer and Jack Rabbits. I've seen enough of people ... killed enough what needed it, and it's time for the big quiet. Maybe ... just maybe, someday I can hunt and fish with my own, fine boy like you. Now ... God Bless You, brave little man, give me a sharp salute and board that people carrier there. Sit safe and close to the driver and carry on,

Little Private, remember now … always look for, and take heed of, "the big quiet." Yeah, get her done, driver … move these good people out … and I'll see you around if you like "The Big Sky Country."

Before I could drop my salute, he was lost among the swirling mass of people. Who was he? Did I imagine him? No matter, because the whole unreal experience was burned in my brain.

DONALD

Damn it all anyway! I meant to get the Marine's address because I would love to write to him and thank him and just … just … I sure hope he has his son someday. I just know he'll be alright living out in Montana among "the Big Quiet." God, a'mighty, it's pitch black tonight … it's okay and I just knew that the Big Marine will make one helluva good Daddy … if he's left alone and the bottle don't get him … later, that night, I had a very sweaty nightmare about finding a huge man frozen to death in a lean-to, clutching a carbine and a quart of sour mash whiskey. There was a huge sign in the dream and it said: "Welcome to the Big Sky Country." I wanted desperately to talk to someone about the dream, but all I got, of course, was, "you just ate too much candy and got too excited." And I went outside and climbed a tree and told the stars: "Bullshit on the candy and being scared downtown … but mainly you … you keep safe, Big Marine, in Montana … you keep safe in peacetime now.

Yes … peacetime now and everybody was hurrying and hustling around to save money to get easy G.I. loans to take advantage of the low-cost housing boom. We were no exception and Daddy's sights, at Momma's urging, were set on a new section called Highland Biltmore. Three bedrooms and a large front yard for football and other games would be a dream come true. Mainly, I wanted a new beginning for my parents, and I quietly worried and wondered if any goal attained – like owning your own home – could bring two people together. Could two personalities, like "oil and water," finally he brought together by achieving something always longed for?

Then ... I got something I had always longed for. I was in Mrs. Moon's class, and the good of that was that she produced and directed the school plays. Mrs. Moon was what Daddy would call, "a pinched, hatchet-faced woman," but she was very nice. Regardless of the fact that she made my life hell by tapping me as room monitor when she left for her cigarette break after every hour. She would come back and lean over my shoulder to see if I had damned any miscreants in my composition book, and the stale smell of her cigarettes would gag me every time. Why was sitting on Papa's lap while he pulled on his Luckies such a soothing, sensual experience, and the smell of Mrs. Moon so God awful? One lunch break, I discussed this with a classmate, the beautiful Nadine Dearman, and we concluded that women were just flat not supposed to smoke in the first place. Looking at Nadine's shiny, raven hair and blue-green eyes, that made perfect sense to me ... yes, Nadine ... just perfect.

The stirrings in me were finally set off like a rocket when Mrs. Moon announced that Nadine would play "Cinderella" and the rest of us had to audition.

DONALD

Finally, I was focused ... totally focused on something that meant everything! I memorized the whole script in one night, and was ready to take on all comers. I never took so long getting dressed for school and then I worried all the way there that I had used too much of Daddy's Vitalis. No matter

... because Nadine told me that she liked boys who were neat and used correct grammar. "Oh ... Lord," I begged, "mouth don't fail me now."

Hey, it didn't and a blessing and a curse fell on me at the same time – I won the role of "the Prince," and all was right with "my Cinderella – the fair Nadine."

But then ... recess came and I had to face the tough and rumbling boys – the ones Momma called "white trash." Huey Burgess marched around Nadine and her girlfriends chanting: "Prince sissy, my fat ass ... Prince Charming, my red neck ass ... Prince Beauty Boy, my Momma's naked patooty!" "My Cinderella" started to speak and then Huey cut loose: "Shut the hell up, Miss Little Perfect Pee Pants!" ... "Huey, you quit it, you stupid tub of guts!"

Well ... sports fans, let's just say that I started rehearsals with an ice pack on a lower lip the size of Delaware. But, of course, as the code demanded, I told Mrs. Moon that I had crashed into the monkey bars playing tag. Somehow, Huey, who played the coachman, with the glass slipper, respected me after that and, after letting me play full tackle football in the mud with his brothers, Huey allowed as how, "I *took a good part* as the Prince," which, where they came from, meant I was a pretty fair country actor.

True or not, I had stood on a stage holding Nadine's perfect hand and had let the world's strongest drug wash through me: APPLAUSE! I thought, "I hope this is all true – that I can become anybody I want to be!" I semi-prayed "let it be true because Junior High is coming up and you can't be a little guy or anybody's baby boy any more."

A year later, I did some pretty difficult character work as "Rip Van Winkle" and sang in the chorus, where I discovered that singing harmony was challenging and fun. Still way too skinny – I also discovered that I could shoot a *two-handed* set-shot with ease on a basketball court. By the beginning of the eighth grade, I also came upon a deep and abiding truth of growing up in the U.S. of A.

DONALD

Now ... no matter how smart or talented you are, or no matter if you could build an Atomic Bomb in science class ... or even if Jesus Christ, Himself, tapped you to be his guide for His second coming – nothing matters in popularity or with girls ... or even with most grown up men in your life – *if you do not make it* in some field of sports!

Nadine and I were something of an "item" now and she already had a lock on head cheerleader, ol' Huey Burgess was assisting the new "cherry coach," as he called him, and pointed to me and said: "That little, skinny Stewart yonder can flat shoot anywhere past mid-court line and he's the same smart peckerwood what made twenty-five foul shots in a row and took my whole week's poke of lunch money off'um me ... and I reckon we shouldn't hold his play-actin' and singin' agin' him."

Of course, old number "26" and, hopefully, number one in Nadine's heart, only got into two games all season. I remember pleading with God, and all other powers, to please let me get stretched up until I was 5'9" in height. Our center was a walloping six feet and I wanted to start with him and feed him on the two-on-three break. Lying on my bed with aching legs on fire with shin splints ... dreaming of cheering crowds and Nadine wearing my letter jacket someday and ... and boom! Daddy opened my door and swayed a bit and announced through some bourbon of celebration:

DADDY

Hey, Little Bunk, we got her – we flat got that pretty, new house in the good section of Highland Biltmore. Hey, by the way, how's your bicycle holdin' up? Keep her in good shape, ol' son, 'cause I've done put you in for a paper route that'll have no less than fifty to sixty customers ... what's the matter, now? We've all got to work hard and pull together. Having our own home is worth every bit of little sacrifices and honest sweat. Just think, Buddy, a new house, new friends, and there you are looking down the barrel at high school ... dumbest, stupidous-assed thing I ever done ... no high school diploma ... Lord save us and bind us and throw us in the ditch where the Devil can't find us. Now ... look here Big Bunkin Boy – Momma's out shopping at Sears and "Rarebuck" ... heh ... heh ... and here – you keep this here grown-man's magazine and ... you ... ah, look at it all you want ... you ... you'll get to feel and know some things that ... that'll make you ... well, you know ... you'll want to ... to ... if you don't know now ... well, you'll feel like you want to ... well do some ... some ... to have some ... well, just go ahead on now –

... And I said simultaneously, as the door shut like a rifle shot, "yeah, I know ... I'll understand someday!"

Well, there I was, gentle people, awash in momentous events and big news – lying there with a forbidden, evil magazine called "Night and Day," which featured semi-naked women in all their voluptuous glory and my shin splints eased up instantly but, within a few moments, I was throbbing elsewhere.

I was so confused ... the unknown staring me down and now Daddy's sex communication and what about a job for me? So, I did what any sensible boy would do when he is utterly adrift and confused – I went to the movies. I galloped along with Wild Bill Elliott as "Red Ryder" and Bobby Blake as "Little Beaver" and, for two hours plus, I was okay with my fast changing world.

After we moved, I busted my hump mowing lawns and carrying groceries home for people just so I could start high school with some serious money for basketball shoes and clothes and, of course, dates of the pure kind with the now fully-developed Nadine. She filled out an Angora sweater to perfection and, having discussed this with the eminent, red-necked philosopher – one Huey "the Barbarian" Burgess, it was concluded that I had personally built Nadine's awesome chest while sitting on the porch most summer nights working on hand development and digital strength for a more perfect set shot. Sure ... ask anybody who made it through to 1949 – you could touch and feel and fondle until you got what was commonly called "the blue balls." You could kiss and even "dry hump," but under no circumstances were you to go "all the way." What a dumb, vacuous phrase ... all the way ... to where? Damn it all – it wasn't that far ... just a few precious inches.

After the heavy session with Nadine and what the guys called "tit construction" dripping sweat in the August humidity of Tidewater, Virginia and listening to mosquitoes so big that they argued over whether to eat or wait to let you fall asleep – I was limping home with my crotch on fire and there was Huey with a hint of saliva slipping out of smacking lips. He noticed my poor condition after Nadine's teasing techniques and the expert "Dr. Burgess" gave me counsel:

HUEY

Now ... you see, ol' son, my big brother, Joe Bob, the one what quit school and joined the Coast Guard right over yonder in Norfolk when he was big for his age at seventeen ... well, he told me all about it. It has to do with pressure – just like a car engine or even like in the cooker in your Momma's kitchen. There has to be release ... a kinda relief-like from all the extra build-up. So ... Brother Joe Bob says nature gives all us men a way of relief. You've got a strong right hand now what with Nadine's sweater plum full of a summer's hard work. So ... there's two ways to go before you bust wide open like Momma's pressure cooker if'un you don't release the pet-cock ... you know, like if the steam builds up too strong – you could have beef stew all over the kitchen walls. Yes ... yes, it's true and can I get an Amen? Now ... there you go – you can use Joe Bob's favorite, the manual technique in a tub of hot, soapy water or ... or ... well if it's flat too painful to wait, you just go over yonder and lift up hard on the ass-end of my Daddy's new Buick. It'll for sure give a body some relief.

And so, by the time I got into the hot, soapy water, I had a terribly sore lower back to go along with my aching genitals. You see, it's not too scientifically or psychologically sound for little, horney guys to go around yanking up on 1948 Buicks.

Now ... transitions, choices, crossroads – we all face or have them thrust upon us. Hell, even ol' Oedipus got in a real mess over the right-of-way at a crossroad. Fathers and sons ... sons and mothers ... and the beat goes on.

Our new house was sparkling and so comfortable because of Momma's splendid work. Everything was humming along fine except I had the sweaty fear again. What initiation faced little guys like me entering high school bound and determined to play basketball? No matter – I went shopping on the Friday before I would take my first five-mile bus ride to Craddock High School that coming Monday.

I was modeling and preparing for my entrance into gym class when the phone rang. I picked up the thick, heavy, ebony thing and remember hearing the words but suddenly, I had no feeling in my legs. It was like the Scarlet Fever had come back on me and I needed to practice walking again. Sweat started to run into my U.S. Keds high tops – I had a job! A paper route for the "Portsmouth Star." Daddy would be home in one hour. And I had to call and confirm my acceptance right after that.

I paced the equivalent of a four-quarter game and sure broke in my new sneakers because, you see, sports fans, "the Star" was the afternoon paper and had to be delivered between 4:00 and 5:30 p.m. Yes ... crossroads-lovers, there I stood, hooked on the proverbial horns.

Daddy's car drove up and he went to the phone pad in the tiny hallway and read my note for what seemed like a half hour and then:

DADDY

I know this is hard, Ol' Bunk ... but you need to think about what you can build this into. Hell, boy, they're building Phase Two of this place right now and, shit son, they'll be at least a hundred more houses to sell your papers to. Now, you've got to call the man at "the Star" after while and tell him your mind ... you know, make a man's decision. It's every day, right after school, Saturday afternoons, and early Sunday mornings – rain or shine, sleet or snow – but she's yours ... your own business to run. "Shore wish I had my own business ... that's the ticket ... hush, Mabel, now. I'll lay it out for the boy, thank you. Now, you can take this job of work and have your own money to do with all through school or turn her down to play that plague-takin' basketball and have *no* spending money. No allowance ... I'll give you piss-all. Now ... for damn sure the ball is in your court. Hell, I was wiring houses with a state license in my pocket when I was seventeen ... no schooling to speak of but, by jumpin' Jesus, I was on my own man – no more my Daddy's slave-farm laborer. A *job* and money got my raggedy ass up and out, and *here I am*! Now you can have it all – school, a job, and your own money what to do with. You're one lucky little guy, ol' son. Wish I had his luck, right, Mabel? You can keep the basketball stuff you bought and I'll pay you back what you spent. Hell, Bunk, you can play basketball all day Sundays – right after church. Right, Momma?

I was hanging in there pretty good and I had a fairly good cap on my tears. Even the picture in my head of the fair Nadine wearing someone else's Craddock Admiral letter jacket didn't cause any screams. I was holding unusually steady until Momma cut loose with, "Praise be to God! Another prayer answered!" Then I lost it:

DONALD

What the hell has church got to do with anything!?! This is very important to me! You've never set foot in a church. Alright ... I'll take the job, but you know why, don't you? Because I have *no* damned choice. Things get real easy for you around here when I have no choice. I'll call the man right now and I'll tell you all one thing for sure – you flat don't have to pay me for this basketball outfit because I earned it and it's all mine ... and you can keep your money. Tithe ten percent on that, Momma.

So ... I had the afternoon job and it's little perk of two free movie passes if you paid your bill in the office by noon on Saturdays. What more could a guy want, right? Choices ... we all have choices ... but who would Nadine choose?

1949 ... the Cold War frigidly raged on and the spectre of mindless, Godless communism loomed daily in the editions of "the Star" that I rolled up and delivered so efficiently seven days a week. Delivering papers can develop into an art form of controlling a bicycle with one or no hands and hurling the tightly wound tubes toward the perfect suburban porches. I had to do it all fast ... I just had to ... wear myself out so I wouldn't think of the guys practicing full-court drills back at the gym. I sold my papers fast too and built my route up to over one hundred customers. Yes ... my money-making business was doing just fine. My independent, little ass was doing just fine ... but who cares about a paper boy?

And then there was school ... ninth grade. This Freshman had duck-tailed hair with a curl pulled down on my forehead, a tee-shirt under a v-neck sweater, a highly envied, rust-colored, soft leather jacket, "draped" or rolled dungaree cuffs and, of course, I wore a pair of righteous penny loafers. At least, I looked like the ball players in my class and I fantasized on the bus ... I was dribbling with a minute to go and Nadine was urging me on in her bulging cheerleader's sweater ... and the crowd was chanting, "Stew-baby ... Stew-baby ... Stew ... going for two ... now let her fly, Stew!?

Ah ... good old fantasy. But I had no room for fantasy, not with English, Algebra I, Latin I, General Science, American History, and a no-nonsense gym class, where you dressed-out and worked hard. Plus, *I would be* the first one in Momma's family to go to college. No pressure at all. Just hump it hard because a scholarship had to be earned. Piece of cake ... except I hated Algebra and Science and the occasional B's struck fear into my heart and put a prayer meeting in Momma's game plan. Yes ... I had a deep fear of failure, but then another crossroad rose up before me and, this time, a hugely positive step was about to be taken.

You see ... my English teacher was one – Mrs. Betty Jane Yarborough, the former B.J. Hathaway of the Rich and Country Clubby Hathaways. She had married her beau at Duke University and he did well as a salesman – so she really didn't have to work. The lady was some sort of freak, I guess, because she purely *loved* teaching and cared about our learning. I was enthralled because it was obvious that Mrs. Yarborough was in her job for all the right reasons. I remember mumbling that I hoped God wasn't joking around and that one day she would go "poof" and there would be the witch from "OZ" cackling on about "Silas Marner."

Can you imagine being fascinated by the workings of the objective and nominative cases ... hypnotized by the incredible architecture of diagramming sentences ... falling into a state of hushed awe when Mrs. Yarborough talked about her "religion of self-expression." The Harbrace Handbook of Grammar became my "Bible."

I had fallen in love, in a way, and then it happened. My idol ... my mentor ... my ... well, she started asking me to stay after school to straighten up and help grade quizzes – highly illegal, I'm sure. I was spellbound by the stories of the Duke English Department and the basketball rivalries with N.C. State and North Carolina. I even got rides home to do my paper route in her shiny, new Pontiac.

Well ... all of this caused much confusion among my peers and one pal, named Vernon Wiggins:

DONALD

Well ... listen to me, Vernon. Come on, now. No more "noogies." Let me start with her hair ... dark as "The Raven's" wings, which she and Mr. Poe introduced to me. Dark blue eyes which flash like sunlight on lagoon ... very expensive silk blouses, and straight well-tailored skirts with seamed stockings on perfectly tapered legs ... gleaming high-heeled pumps pulling the muscles of her calfs as she diagrams sentences as Rembrandt might have painted ... her skin is like cream risen to where all else seems milky and watery. All the other classrooms smell musty like Algebra, but Mrs. Yarborough's smells ... well, like her! English soap ... Yeardley, I think, like my Uncle Horace brought Momma home from London in 1945. And now, in my opinion, no woman should use any hand lotion but Jergens ... ever. Every trip from the blackboard has a ritual stop at the large lotion bottle on her lemon-oiled, polished desk. And she uses some exotic shampoo, which I've never got the courage to ask her about. Let me put it this way, guys – this lady would be committing a "grievous fault," as Billy Shakespeare said it, if she ever desecrated her neck and shoulders with perfume. And when she raises a shade at the window and the sunlight hits just right – the outline of her brazziere can cause any guy to mis-conjugate a verb. A couple of times, she has run her perfect hand through my hair or touched my shoulder to the rhythm of a poem I've been reading aloud and I have to slip my notebook over my lap to keep my tight jeans or corduroys from bursting open. Now ... try to believe this – this elegant lady loves Howard Johnson hot dogs and, at least twice a week, we get two each with large Coca-Colas with lemon and shaved ice. Now ... mix the sinful smell of that with the heavenly air of Mrs. Betty Jane Yarborough, all captured in a brand new Pontiac with real leather seats and, guys, you could pass flat out from overloaded circuits and pounding blood vessels ... One day she recited a poem by some foreign guy named Dylan Thomas and it sounded like warm honey cascading over the lip of a porcelain pitcher – if honey could ever make such a sound and ... SNAP! Hey, you guys, you can come to now, and no, Vernon Wiggins, I had not gotten laid yet!

Mrs. Yarborough loved bowling and basketball and she and her husband, Graham, took me with them and I discovered that I was pretty good with the duck pins. I was pretty confused, though, when Mr. Yarborough missed a spare. He would stamp his foot and whirl back to his Coca-Cola and Nabs and cross his legs just like Momma did when she didn't get her way with Daddy. They took me to Williamsburg, Virginia, to watch the Duke Blue Devils go through the lowly William and Mary Indians like a dose of salts. Graham was passionate about his Blue Devils but, as we drove home, I had never seen a man use his hands and wrists so limply as he gestured or drove the big, old Pontiac. All the way back, Mrs. Yarborough sat in the middle and she had her left hand on Graham's inner thigh and the other on my knee and I talked incessantly about colleges and various writers – anything to keep from screaming, "I'm going crazy in this confusion! What's a man!?! What's love!"! What's marriage!?!" And, just before we got to my house, I said out loud: "I bet God is leaning back in his big chair, up yonder, and saying ... you'll understand someday ... someday, you'll know."

What I did know was that Nadine was being birdogged by a popular football player and I just had to participate in some sport. Another Duke graduate was the track coach and he was looking for cross country runners now and guys who could run the mile come Spring. Hell, my skinny self could run all day and deliver papers at the end of that. Coach Riggs let me use gym class to stretch and run endless laps and soon, I was ready for our special challenge meets on Saturday mornings.

DONALD

On a crisp, fall day, we ran against Granby High from Norfolk and all the football players, cheerleaders, and a few teachers and students, were in the stands by high noon because our earlier ten mile run across country roads and byways would finish with the last mile kicking around our school track. Some called it "the kick and bust ass – heartbreak mile." Nadine had promised to be there and, as we lumbered through the gates, I prayed, "Legs don't fail me now."

Boom! On to the track and me in fifth place. Just as I finished the first lap, I caught Nadine sitting next to a "Big A", maroon sweater and broke stride a little. Screw it! And I moved into fourth place on the far turn and, as I pumped toward the grandstand area, my legs gained strength and, just then I felt a snap! No muscle pull ... no, nothing puny like that ... just ... oh, God! In front of Nadine, God, and everybody – my jock strap broke! And over the screams and hard laughter, I heard Coach Riggs yelling, "Run, you skinny-assed fool, kick her home!" God knows, I tried ... blinded by scalding tears and rounding the near turn, all I could hear was the whole basketball team screaming, "Hey, Sweetheart ... hey, baby doll, you lost your *Kotex* ... do your *Kotex* kick, Baby!" ... I don't remember the pain when my knees hit the cinders 'cause I flat passed out. Coach Riggs picked me up in his arms and, the first face I saw was Mrs. Yarborough and she was working with Coach's pocket knife to cut off the flapping jock strap. With her coat over me,

I lifted my head toward the whole team bench and there was Nadine, bent over with laughter and burrowing her head into a co-captain's sweater. Our school had finished first ... second ... and I was third – a triumph! And maybe a school letter ... but my life was over right then and there. "Sports, my ass," I sobbed! And then threw up all over Mrs. Yarborough's English, flannel coat.

Momma was shopping and Daddy was basking with the boys in a bourbon and boiled crabs feast near Suffolk – so we were alone when the Pontiac stopped in our driveway. The numbed silence was broken with, "May I come in?" Of course, and I gave Mrs. Yarborough some ice tea and showered and changed. I tried to eat some saltines for my stomach and, out of the blue, she said, "Donald, just like when I found out about my husband, Graham, being ... well ... different and deeply troubled, and divorce out of the question in my family ... we just ... well, please remember this, 'That which does not kill you makes you stronger.'" Hell, I didn't understand her marriage anymore than my parents staying together. And then she kissed me very tenderly on the lips. I didn't get excited or horny ... I just felt relieved that someone understood my confusion and pain.

Then from a shoulder bag, out came two books – brand new and with an inscription that read, "People can hurt you – God can sometimes turn his back or laugh from above – but the poets endure. They are the ones who know ... know how life is or how it should be and sometimes even the difference between the two. Love to the son I'll never have – always, Betty Jane."

And with that, she went to the door, turned, and said, "Learn the poem on page 56 and pick out any one of Romeo's monologues because you're going to perform in the Language, Arts, Speech, and Drama assembly right before Thanksgiving."

"Oh, please stay," I begged, but she had to go visit her mother-in-law and her face fell because, written all over it, was an enormous emptiness. I tried to ask but was too shaky and, just before the Pontiac pulled out, she patted my hand and said, "Remember, roads taken or not taken ... and of all sad words of tongue and pen – the saddest of these are what might have been."

Right then and there, I knew for certain that I would bust my brains and ass to make Mrs. B.J. proud of me. And, by God, college for this semi-poor boy was going to be a reality!

I studied Edgar Allan Poe and *Romeo and Juliet* every free moment I had. Luckily, iambic pentameter flowed through me easily and my slight stutter and diction improved daily. Wrongly or rightly, I chose "Annabel Lee" and Romeo's death speech. Momma became a critic and deemed my choices, "gloomy and doomy." And then, when I threw over the Twenty-Third Psalm, she lost it and yelled, "Is Mrs. Yarborough pushing her will on my shining star?!?" I backed silently to the door, and then calmly replied, "I'm not even going to answer that – I'd rather go run five miles than try to answer that." And so I did.

They were choosing sides for a full-court game, when I burst through the gym doors. Coach Riggs signaled for me to Captain the team to take on the winner of the first game. Theron, a young, beefy football player yelled, "Hey, Kotex Queen, pick me, Sweetie-Pie." As I turned, Theron pulled a stick match and struck it on his dungarees to scare me and snap! The fiery match head flew directly in my left eye. Numbness ... then a sudden blindness ... then my right eye focused in again and I saw a softball bat in the corner ... "Hey, Little Man, I didn't mean it" ... the first blow hit Theron around the collar bone and then the chase was on ... as the searing, white hot pain finally speared me, I screamed, "Hey, God! I'm getting stronger – I'm getting there!" Just before oblivion hit, I heard two voices: "Jesus Christ a'mighty, he's gone crazy ... Match burn of the eye ... Little Kotex has got a right to go snakeshit."

If Coach Riggs had been fifteen minutes later getting downtown to the specialist, my nickname would have changed to "ol' one-eye." It would be a while before the bandages came off and I would know.

I remember shocking Momma and Daddy when the first pain pills were off by shouting, "Damn it, God All Mighty! I turned yellow from a sulfur drug for Scarlet Fever and now a sulfur burn of the eye! No wonder Catholics fear purgatory so much!"

I studied "Romeo" and Poe for three hours at a pop and rolled in agony for one hour because I could only take a pill every four hours. It was easy to understand how addicts and junkies were born. I hoped I wouldn't turn out like ol' Edgar Allan Poe and blind in one eye to boot. At least I didn't try Daddy's bourbon, but I considered it.

I didn't know what consideration to give when Theron, the sensitive match-striker, came over and sat staring out the windows as he:

THERON

Ah ... y'all see ... ah ... I'm supposed to go to Wake Forest on a football scholarship in about ... well, 'bout two years, and I want you to ... well, to know that I'd give ... I'd give it all ... you know, give her up just to know you'll see again by next Friday when ... you know, if you could manage it – I would shore 'preciate it if ... if ... well, you think you might could sit with me in church tomorrow? I ain't prayed in quite a spell except last September in the huddle when we needed six yards to score a big'un. So ... I'd shore like to pray beside you at church like ... you know, so as to ... like we could be ... hey, please grow up strong and do it quick so you can whip this bully's ignorant ass. Well ... I've got to ... well, go on down the road for now.

Oh ... and bless all y'all what are here in this house.

The pill wore off just as Theron hit the porch and I sucked wind hard and yelled, "I'll see you Sunday, eleven o'clock, tenth pew, left side." I thought to myself ... learning things in this old world comes to us in the strangest ways sometimes. I didn't think I needed a preacher or a sermon, but if Theron did, that was fine too, and I'd be there for him. No ... for both of us ... Amen.

Before they took the bandage off on Thursday, I thought, "It's almost 1950! What a decade ... what an incredible time to live in! But I hope I don't have to do the next ten years with only one eye. But, hey, wearing a black patch just might be "cool" for the 1950's."

The unveiling finally took place and I was still blessed with sight. Oh ... the old left eye might drift a bit when tired, but what the hell:

DONALD

I'm going up on that stage tomorrow and do my pieces no matter what! Something stirred in me from the fifth grade "Cinderella" play and ... and ... well, screw the letter sweaters in basketball or track ... if I can do Poe and Billy Shakespeare and ... Lord, save me, get it right – they can bronze my broken jock strap and nail it over the gymnasium door! Hey ... sports fans, I can see! Thanks, Doc ... thanks, Momma for the nursing ... thanks ol' soothing hands Daddy, and Coach, you're the best ... and Mrs. B.J. Yarborough, I love you, I truly do ... and I know one thing for sure – I love the bloody, but unbowed, English language!

Performance day was on and the auditorium was packed. My fear of failure hit hard when the senior forensics competition went first. There were some great speeches and one heated and controversial debate about what was going on with Gen. Douglas MacArthur, as Pro-Consul of Japan, and his opinions on Indo-China, wherever the hell that was. Then some serious points were raised about the United States getting caught up in "A barbaric and dangerous conflict" in some place called Korea. All I said to myself was: "We couldn't possibly go to war again, so soon ... hell, that would be crazy ... as Billy Ray would have said – "Dunnud, that would be plum crazy."

War, my ass, I had results of a blood feud between the Montagues and the Capulets to deal with, and Verona's problems I understood. The Koreans could have Korea and, if not – what's the harm of a little more land for the Chinese?

And speaking of war, I fought a terrible "beachhead" and something worse than a raging fever. A terrible invasion hit me: flop sweat! It poured down my corduroys and made my new V-neck clammy and sticky. Mrs. Yarborough ruffled my hair and said: "Forget those words – 'Oh, what might have been' and go out there for *you* ... find the *real* you. And remember, your contrast ... show your range."

"You damned right," I said, and squeezed her slender, lotioned hand.

Contrast ... contrast and ... well, Poe was, in essence a Southerner so ... hell, so am I. And Mrs. B.J.'s coaching with the Shakespeare has been like ... well, a find conductor, and for some reason, I prayed as I walked center stage: "Lord, let me give something, let me communicate and, therefore, I will receive ... and then I'll have an Amen."

ANNABEL LEE

It was many and many a year ago,
    In a kingdom by the sea.
That a maiden there lived whom you may know

By the name of Annabel Lee;
And this maiden she lived with no other thought
    Than to love and be loved by me.

I was a child and she was a child,
    In this kingdom by the sea;
But we loved with a love that was more than love –
    I and my Annabel Lee;
With a love that the winged seraphs of heaven
    Coveted her and me.

And this was the reason, that, long ago,
    In this kingdom by the sea,
A wind blew out of a cloud, chilling
    My beautiful Annabel Lee;
So that her high-born kinsmen came
    And bore her away from me,
To shut her up in a Sepulchre
    In this kingdom by the sea.

The angels, not half so happy in heaven,
    Went envying her and me –
Yes! – that was the reason (as all men know
    In this kingdom by the sea)
That the wind came out of a cloud by night,
    Chilling and killing my Annabel Lee.

But our love was stronger by far than the love
    Of those who were older than we –
    Of many far wiser than we –
And neither the angels in heaven above,
    Nor the demons down under the sea,
Can ever dissever my soul from the soul,
    Of the beautiful Annabel Lee,

For the moon never beams without bringing me dreams
    Of the beautiful Annabel Lee;
And the stars never rise but I see the bright eyes

>   Of the beautiful Annabel Lee;
> And so, all the night-tide, I lie down by the side
> Of my darling, my darling, my life and my bride,
>   In her sepulchre there by the sea –
>   In her tomb by the sounding sea.

Some of the guys in the audience had to be quieted by Coach Riggs. One football player was thrown out when he said too loudly: "Hey, Little Kotex, go on crawl in the tomb with her 'cause you flat can't run!"

Nadine Dearman suddenly stood up and stared down a whole bunch of the jocks. Then I did something completely crazy. I gestured for her to come up on stage and, as I pushed a debate table to center, Nadine joined me. I whispered to her and she lay down and crossed her arms over her beautiful chest and closed her heavenly blue-green eyes:

ROMEO

> How oft when men are at the point of death
> Have they been merry! which their keepers call
> A lightning before death: O, how may I
> Call this a lightning? O my love! my wife!
> Death, that hath suck'd the honey of thy breath,
> Hath had no power yet upon thy beauty:
> Thou art not conquer'd; beauty's ensign yet
> Is crimson in thy lips and in thy cheeks,
> And death's pale flag is not advanced there.
> Tybalt, liest thou there in thy bloody sheet?
> O, what more favour can I do to thee,
> Than with that hand that cut thy youth in twain
> To sunder his that was thine enemy?
> Forgive me, cousin! Ah, dear Juliet,
> Why art thou yet so fair? shall I believe
> That unsubstantial death is amorous,
> And that the lean abhorred monster keeps
> Thee here in dark to be his paramour?

For fear of that, I still will stay with thee;
And never from this palace of dim night
Depart again. Here, here will I remain
With worms that are thy chamber-maids; O, here
Will I set up my everlasting rest,
And shake the yoke of inauspicious stars
From this world-wearied flesh. Eyes, look your
last! Arms, take your last embrace! and, lips, O you
The doors of breath, seal with a righteous kiss
A dateless bargain to engrossing death!
Come, bitter conduct, come, unsavoury guide!
Thou desperate pilot, now at once run on
The dashing rocks thy sea-sick weary bark!
Here's to my love! – O true apothecary!
Thy drugs are quick. – Thus with a kiss I die.

We bowed together and walked off into Mrs. Yarborough's waiting arms. Her tears had sure stained her silken blouse and my sweat was still pouring. But, what the hell, I had the two best ladies in the world – one on each arm.

Momma missed my performance because she had gone to work as a receptionist for two lady doctors a few blocks from our house. Brother Lee was now in the first grade and doing beautifully and besides, we desperately needed the money. You see, Daddy's drinking had escalated to serious proportions and he had quit the Navy yard, worked for the Sunshine Biscuit Company briefly, then became a Deputy to our drunken Sherriff – quit and went back to the Navy yard and raged horribly about what his status should be. One Saturday night, I had to lock all three of us in the car until Daddy passed out.

No more "oil and water" – it was now fire and icy gasoline, if there could be such a thing. Something had to change – there had to be relief, so:

DONALD

Listen now ... I know there's never been a divorce in either family but, please will you both think about it? Daddy, you can live the life you want and come and go as you please – have your own apartment or stay with old Sheriff Upchurch. Lee and I will come to see you. You don't have to give us much money. Just ... just ... listen, you could get help for the drinking and ... not just for us, but for *you*. Where's our good ol' soothing, healing Daddy ... where's the hard-working, trouble-shooting, A-one electrician when your belly's full of bourbon!?! Where's the *real* you? Bad grammar, but that *ain't* you, Daddy! No ... Momma, you keep quiet for now. Daddy, don't just walk out now – nothing's settled or ever talked about ... no ... no. We may never have a chance to talk all this out again ... no, don't quit on it, come on, let's talk ... no! It's alright, Lee ... it's alright, Little Brother. I'm not mad and he'll be back ... and no, we're not just Momma's sissy, Baptist boys – Daddy doesn't really mean that. We're the Stewart Brothers and mainly, by God, we love books and school and we'll be alright ... we will ... we have to be. There's a plan working ... somewhere ... right, God? There's a plan working here?!?

Separately, I asked my parents why they got married in the first place and, more importantly, why they stayed married. Momma, of course, said she reckoned Daddy was simply "her Christian cross to bear," and Daddy kinda looked at me like I was a snake. Hey ... I'm still confused here, sports fans, I'm raised on a battleground; Mrs. Yarborough has to stay with her limp wrested and "troubled" Graham, and Momma's now working for two lady doctors who roomed together all through school and are, according to Momma, "the very best of loving friends." Yah ... is it time yet? Can it be time now? Can this be the famous *"someday"* I'll know!?!

Then one freakishly mild, Winter day, Daddy and I were alone on the back porch. He loved to just look at the area where, come Spring, he'd have another fine, vegetable garden. Daddy was awfully shakey, but he finally talked to me:

DADDY

Son ... give me a couple of those ice cubes outta your R.C. glass, will you? Yeah ... that's the ticket – sometimes ol' J.T.S. Brown needs the sour mash cooled down a mite ... you know, something has kinda creeped up on me now. Prentice, my oldest brother, dropped dead plowing at high noon, they say, and Q.J.'s got cancer of the throat and they're butcherin' on him like a hog in Raleigh. Now baby-brother, Glen, is on the run – screwin' every skirt in sight and winning his bar drinks with a six-inch punch ... and here I am ... just goin' to work, taking all manner of crap from no' account bosses who couldn't go to the outhouse alone without getting' it in their hair ... oh, I know I got two good boys who might make something of theirselves some day. This house your Momma tends so special, is sure a comfort and no man's ever eaten better food. Hell, I've gone from 147 pounds to new 'bout 220 in sixteen years of married life ... and we've all got our health now. Shootfire, I ain't even too far in debt ... and ... and none of it is enough or works for me. It's like when your car hits the ice and you keep trying to pull the wheel the other way ... you ain't ever gonna stop the slide if you keep pullin' against the true course of the car. It's a fact of nature. I know ... 'cause I went against my own nature ... I know it. *That's* what you got to *know*, son. Who you *really are*! What your true center, as a man, is. We should get that from our Grandfathers and our Fathers, but times have changed so fast – too damned fast in this "baby" of a country of ours. You see, I was never shown how to do a friggin' thing by my old man ... just tote and chop cotton and pull stumps ... just be a nigger-to-the-plow and a field hand to the hoe. That just don't cut it, ol' son. Hell, us boys weren't even allowed to eat at the table with the grown ups ... we heard no stories ... learned no legends or tales. Now ... you can't say I ever kept you from my right hand at the table, boy. No, sir-ree-bob, you were always there. Now ... you see, the Apaches and Cheyenne Indians and such got it all right. When they neared their manhood, like you just done, Indian boys were ready for initiation – kinda an entry – like into being a man. Their boys go into trials-like and have to survive tests and challenges, and then they come back with their *center*. You know, their self-confidence. They know how to think and to do and behave like a centered man – a man in tune with his world. Not like some guitar with busted strings ... you see, that's me – just plum out of tune with busted strings ... I got married before I knew piss-all – I just wanted to show my Daddy that I could land a clean, decent girl ... and your Momma did find me exciting and handsome, I reckon, and she just knew she could make me into her dream; a fine, kinda neutered, Christian man! Bull hockey! Remember now, nobody can *change* nobody and shouldn't even try.

Anyway ... you get your full education now, and I'm sorry I never helped you outta your boyhood and into ... well, into wherever you headin' ... you see, now there's them "rumors of war" again ...

yeah, risin' up again, and we're sure primed to get in the middle of this North Korean-South Korean mess ... Puzon ... 38th parallel ... hell, some think MacArthur wants to be emperor of all them yellow people! Well ... he can have 'em all save six. You see, I had my chance to do something special ... maybe a hero or go from Corpsman to medical school 'cause I've got the healin' touch, son ... but the good war didn't want me, and now I'll miss this test of manhood and courage too. Remember now, it's never enough to just keep on a 'keepin' on, like Momma's preachers say, you got to *know* what you want and go, by God, get her done! ... you've got the equipment there – right there in your head and heart ... and if I could just cut myself some slack – I'd say I done the best I could with the equipment I had ...

I love you, Bunk ... now go on and do your homework, but before you leave me, let me hold that perfect-ironed pocket handkerchief your Momma gave you this morning ... go ahead on ... go ahead on now ... please just go ahead on, my son.

And I did ... I surely did. I went right to my notebook and wrote my plans ... my options ... challenges for the college scholarships, and I added: "I resolve to go with my strengths to find my center – no matter how scary the journey is!" Oh ... and I added: "If I can stay out of some crazy war in Korea." Then I looked at my calendar and, I'll be damned, I had made *resolutions* and it was December 31, New Year's Eve – 1949 ... and another decade had been spent.

www.ingramcontent.com/pod-product-compliance
Lightning Source LLC
Chambersburg PA
CBHW021025090426
42738CB00007B/904